Fun With
Magnets

by Lynne Anderson

Table of Contents

What Is Magnetism? 2

How Can You Use a Magnet to
Take the Iron Out of Cereal? 10

How Can You Make a Toy Using Magnets? 14

Glossary and Index 20

What Is Magnetism?

Have you ever hung a picture on a refrigerator door? Have you ever rung a doorbell or used a computer? If you answered yes, then you have used the property of **magnetism**. Magnets are very important materials. They are in many of the objects you use every day.

▲ A computer is one of many machines that use magnets.

▲ Magnets come in different shapes and sizes. Some magnets are in the shape of a horseshoe. Other magnets are long, straight bars. Still others are small, round disks.

All magnets have some things in common. They all have two ends, or **poles**. One pole is called the south pole. The other is called the north pole. The poles of a magnet always come in pairs. You cannot have a north pole without a south pole. You also cannot have a south pole without a north pole.

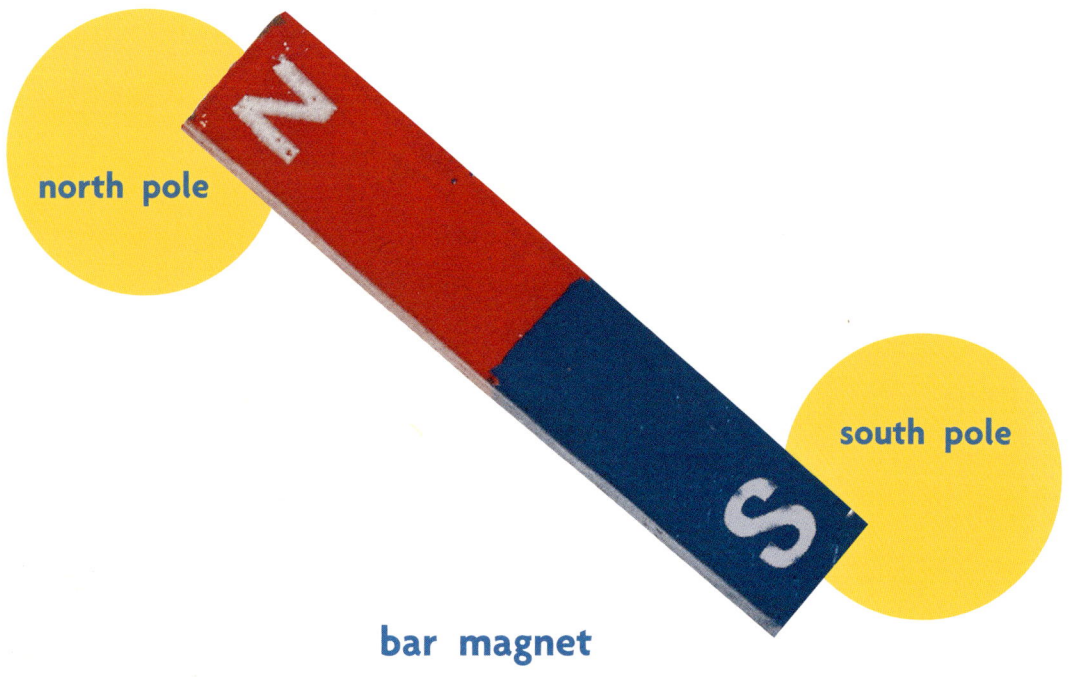

north pole

south pole

bar magnet

What Makes a Magnet a Magnet?

Imagine breaking a magnet into smaller and smaller pieces. Each piece would also be a magnet. Now imagine breaking one of those magnets into pieces so small they cannot be seen. These tiny pieces are called **atoms**. The atoms in a magnet are arranged in a special way. They line up pole to pole. This is what gives a magnet its magnetism!

The atoms in a magnet line up.

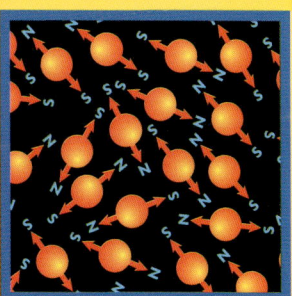

The atoms in a nonmagnet do not line up.

When the poles of two magnets are brought together, they either **attract** or **repel** each other. When two south poles are brought together, the magnets repel each other. Two north poles also repel each other. When a north pole and a south pole are brought together, the magnets attract each other.

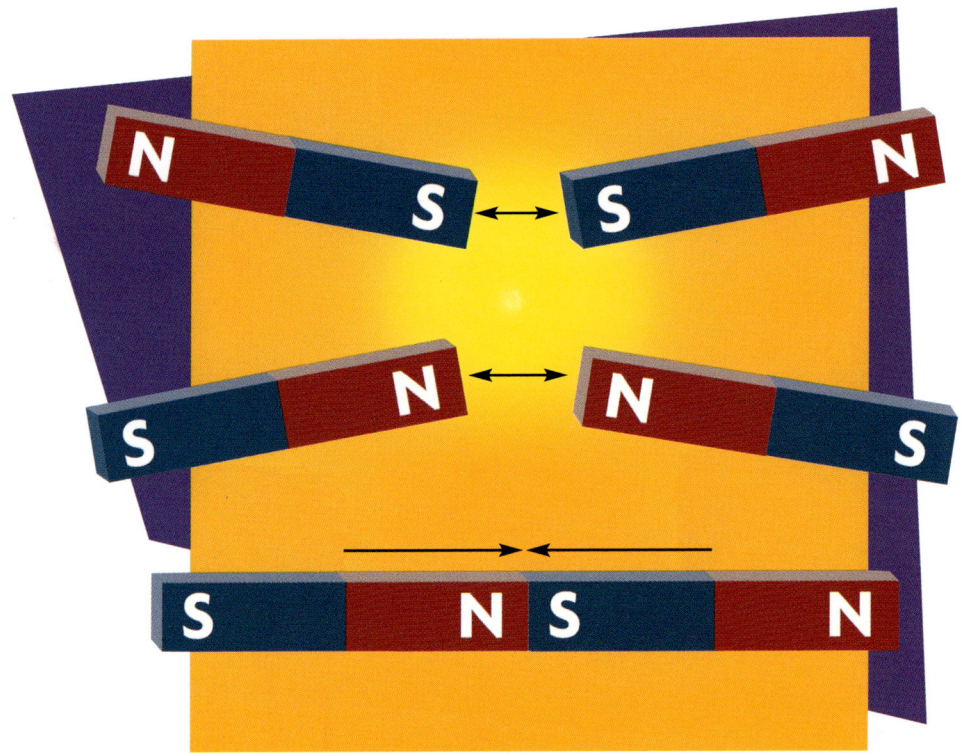

What else do magnets attract? They attract objects that are made of **iron**. Objects such as paper clips, nails, and pins all contain iron.

Paper clips, nails, and pins aren't magnets. But they all act like magnets when a magnet is brought near them. This is because the magnet can make the atoms in iron materials line up. When the magnet is removed, the atoms move out of line. The iron material no longer acts like a magnet.

Why are the paper clips being picked up by the magnet?

Magnets cannot attract all materials. Objects made of such materials as plastic, copper, wood, or glass are not attracted by magnets. Magnets cannot make the atoms in these materials line up.

Object	Material	Is Attracted by a Magnet
	rubber	no
	plastic	no
	iron	yes

To Attract or Not to Attract?

Collect some everyday objects to experiment with. They can include the objects listed in the chart. Use a magnet to test each object. Make a chart like the one shown to record your observations.

Object	Material	Is Attracted by a Magnet
	wood	no
	steel	yes
	brass	no

How Can You Use a Magnet to Take the Iron Out of Cereal?

You have just learned that magnets attract iron. Did you know there is iron in cereal and other foods, such as red meat? Iron is an important mineral. Your body needs it to stay strong and healthy.

Did You Know?

Magnets can be used to separate iron from mixtures. Powerful magnets are used at junkyards to separate iron products from other garbage so that they can be recycled.

To see how well magnets attract iron, you can try to "pull" the iron out of a bowl of cereal!

What you will need:

bowl of iron-fortified cereal

strong bar magnet

water

paper towels

Step 1 Pour water into the bowl of cereal. Let the cereal sit for 5 to 10 minutes until it becomes very soggy.

Step 2 While you are waiting, wipe the magnet with a paper towel. Make sure that the poles of the magnet are clean.

You know the magnet is clean when you do not see any black specks on the paper towel.

Step 3 When the cereal is well soaked, stir the magnet through the water for about 30 seconds.

Step 4 Use a paper towel to wipe the magnet again. What do you see? What do you think happened?

The black specks that you see are bits of iron from the cereal. The iron was attracted to the magnet and was pulled out of the cereal!

How Can You Make a Toy Using Magnets?

In this activity, you can have fun playing with attraction and repulsion.

What you will need:

- construction paper
- glue
- pencil or marker
- rubber band
- 2 corks
- scissors
- strong magnet
- glass or plastic dish
- pin
- 1 cup of water

Step 1 Fold a piece of construction paper in half. Draw a boat on the paper. Draw a small rectangle below the bottom of the boat to make a tab. The tab will be used to attach the boat to the cork.

Step 2 Cut the boat out of the folded paper. You should have two identical paper boats when you are finished. Fold up the tabs at the bottom of each boat and set the boats aside.

Step 3 Rub the pin in one direction over the magnet about 30 times. Remember to rub in the same direction each time. This action will magnetize the pin.

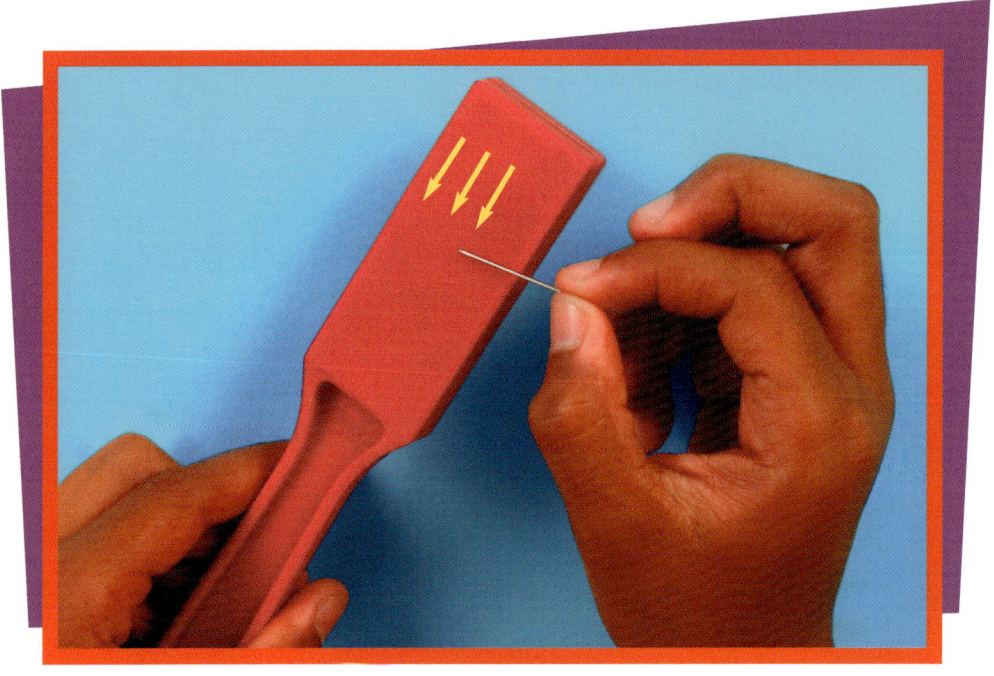

▲ Because the atoms in iron materials line up easily, you can make iron materials magnetic by stroking them with a strong magnet. The atoms won't stay lined up forever. Your iron material will lose its magnetic properties.

Step 4 Put glue on one of the boats. Then place the magnetized pin in the center of the boat with the point facing down.

Step 5 Now glue the boats together with the pin in place between them.

Step 6 Put a rubber band around the corks to connect them. Then glue the folded rectangular tabs onto the corks.

Step 7 Fill the pan with water and float the boat on the water.

Put the magnet near your boat. What happens? Why does this happen?

▲ Use the magnet to make your boat "sail" through the water.

Glossary

atom (AT-um): the smallest unit of matter

attract (uh-TRAKT): to pull

iron (EYE-urn): a metal that can be attracted by a magnet

magnetism (MAG-nuh-tiz-um): a property of matter; the ability to attract or repel certain materials

pole (POHL): the end of a magnet where attraction or repulsion is the strongest

repel (ree-PEL): to push

Index

atoms	5, 7–8, 16
attract	6–11, 13, 14
iron	7–8, 10–13, 16
poles	4–6, 12
repel	6, 14